A Smattering of Smitter

A smatter, do
A smitter, gc ... .

A smatter sometimes clatters
A smitter often glitters

These words you may think phoney
A load of old boloney

But the thing that made you groan
Was invented by Ms Jones

Now you know your smitterings
Were you really listening?

Christening this little book
Hair on end a while she took

Nearly drove her hubby mad
Now she's finished I'm so glad

For the words that caused vexation
Only mean a
compilation!

The Cartoon

In the mid-1960s Don Thompson drew cartoons for the *Daily Sketch* (newspaper). He very kindly agreed to produce an illustration of Katie at her writing desk.

Cartoon: Katie hard at work on her book
© Don Thompson (2019)

Katie Myers

DER 1153 B

SONGS FOR SINGING

CATHY WILKIN

(Cathy Wilkin)

With Roy Gibson - Organ Denny Bell - Drums

Dave Venus - Guitar

PRODUCER FRANK WAPPAT

"My song has come home, and to hold that old recording in my hands was an amazing feeling. The emotions were just incredible as I'd not heard it for over 30 years at least!"

Above: The record label of Katie's own recording of *Songs for Singing.*

Statutory Stutterings

Copyright © 2019 Katie Myers
ISBN 978-0-244-79823-9

First edition August 2019.

This amazing journey into publishing
was written by Katie and
put together by
her Dream Team.

Author contact: kt.smat01smits@gmail.com

Formatted at Fynevue in England.

No lamp oil was spilt in the making of this book.

Proudly printed and distributed via www.lulu.com

Contents

Dedication

This book is dedicated to my mum and dad, Margaret and Jim.

You took me into your hearts and lives when I was 4 months old. We became a family on 24 December 1951. Your loving care and devotion gave me the happiest childhood, for which I'm eternally grateful. Without your support and great good sense, not forgetting humour, I couldn't have become the woman I am today.

I know you would have been overjoyed with the publication of this book of poetry and prose. Even though you're no longer here, this is just for you my beautiful adopted parents.

***

Acknowledgements

John Chenery without whose help this book would never have seen the light of day! My sincere thanks for your help; advice and guidance through the self-publishing maze. A friend I've never met, you have given time with generosity to someone who couldn't do the job herself. One of life's gentlemen!

Writing friends: **Gladys Taylor**. Thank you for a blush making foreword; your help, support and editing of my writing over the years. Invaluable. **Elisabeth S** giving of your knowledge, insight and critique when needed, a wonderful assist. Both of you have aided my learning and growth, and now I've gained the confidence to put this book together, something I thought would never happen!

Liz Jones poem analyst, editor and section sorter. Your mad ideas and madcap chats have encouraged me to get this together rather than flounder like a landed fish. A fabulous friend and all-round nut case, you're a joy to know.

Candie Doy thank you for proof-reading my prose; gathering the word count, giving me honest critique and total encouragement. Oh, and did I mention the laughs? Here's to many more, and don't think your work is over!

Best friend **Pat Tinmouth**, the sister I would have chosen. Without you the sun would hide behind the clouds. You encourage me through tough times, and we laugh over mad things. Thank you for always being there, making me believe in me.

Vivienne Mitchinson for providing me with the perfect photo from my wedding day. Being such a wonderful amateur photographer, it was difficult to know which one to choose, but that one got the thumbs up. Thanks for the happy times.

Bob Lyons, another wonderful person, who reunited me with the *Songs for Singing* single, which I wrote and recorded when I was 24! Hearing that part of my past made me feel emotions I haven't experienced in a long time. I'm so grateful to be able to listen to it again. A huge and sincere thank you from my heart.

Don Thompson for creating an amazing cartoon of me hard at work with all my necessities beside me! You're a star.

My fantastic son **Richard**, we annoy the hell out of each other, then laugh like lunatics over shared humour. You've grown into a wise and precious man, love you so much. I especially enjoy your incisive suggestions and comments, thank you a million times.

Brian, my devoted hubby. We've weathered some storms, but love keeps us together. You encourage me in everything I do, always there to pick up the pieces, share a laugh, soothe my fears and drive me to the next hospital appointment. Not forgetting your Spag Bol, which is second to none!

Finally, to every treasured friend who has thrown out a crumb of encouragement, I love and thank you always.

***

Foreword

From the moment I heard Katie's bright smile and friendly chat in an online room for vision impaired persons I felt uplifted.

As time passed, we shared creative writings.

Her ability to bring feelings to the surface in simple words has always hooked me in - I want to keep reading, be it haiku to free verse to expressive prose.

In this her first book you will travel with her through life writings, laugh at comical nonsenses, and cry as she touches you in the deepest moments of raw emotion.

You will be asking for more from Katie after you read this, her first collection of very personal creative works.

Gladys Taylor
BA (Hons) Open University

***

Introduction

My journey into poetry began after we were given the shattering diagnosis that I'd be blind by the time I was in my late teens.

Aged 10, standing at the bus stop with my mum, I remember sobbing because at least it wasn't going to happen for a few years yet. The news seemed to kick start me trying to make pictures with words, and now think of it like a movie in the mind. If you ever listened to a radio play, all you have is voices to make you 'see' what's going on, well that's what I wanted to do with my poetry, and my short stories too.

I wrote a poem about meandering rivers, long grasses and wild ponies. They were the first words written after we came back from that appointment. Standing next to my mum's chair, I handed over my notebook, eagerly watched her read it, and was completely puzzled when she burst into tears.

"It's beautiful, love," was all she could manage to say.

She asked if she could keep it, and the image of that piece of paper becoming crinkled with handling, as she read it over and over, eyes filled with love and sorrow, still haunts me.

Once the girls at our secondary school found out about my ability, I was 'commissioned' to write a poem for whoever their favourite crush was at the time.

Later, at sixteen, I began writing gospel songs for a group we formed when I was in the Salvation Army. Again, I enjoyed the whole process of words and the feelings they could evoke.

Just this year, I tried to dredge up the words I'd written so long ago, and now saved them to remind me of those times with the girls, and our four guitars, us singing our hearts out at various Salvation Army halls. Sadly, time erodes memory and I could only remember three out of at least half a dozen that were written at the time.

In 1974, a new gospel programme began on *BBC Radio Newcastle* called *Songs for Singing*. So, I sat down and wrote a song reflecting the name of the show.

Contacting the DJ, I offered him that one, along with the others that I'd written for our little group. To my utter amazement he got me to record *Songs for Singing*, and the chorus was played as the introduction to the programme every Sunday for several years.

That led to me appearing at Newcastle's City Hall and around the region in different churches and other venues when he took the show on the road. The thrill of hearing an audience reaction to my singing something I'd composed never left me, so I continued writing, although not on a regular basis.

In 1981, I did a course in sound recording and journalism where my writing really started to take off. Alongside the poetry, short stories began evolving. By this time my sight had been non-existent for several years, and I found myself trying more and more to create pictures with words. Recording my thoughts and ideas on cassette tapes was the only way of working as I didn't own a PC at the time.

Then in the mid-90s someone gave me some information that changed my world. There was a charity down on the south coast where an application could be made to obtain funding for a PC of my own. This was exciting. A social worker had to uphold the claim. We filled in and sent off the necessary paperwork, then we waited. Three months later, I whooped around the room when I got word back that my request had been granted - I became the proud owner of a beautiful new laptop.

Then a second grant from a local charity enabled me to buy JAWS screen reader which allowed me to hear everything I typed. Once I got to grips with the keystrokes, how to save and create files and folders, there was no stopping me. No internet for me back then, so no distractions.

Wanting to put something back, Dad and I organised an evening's entertainment at a local club. We made it fancy dress and were surprised at how many people turned up to support us and the charity. It was a great evening, alongside a disco there was a fantastic singer who was manager of our local pub. At the end of the event, we'd made over £200 to send back to the charity who'd gifted my laptop. They were delighted, and I was able to carry on writing.

The next biggest boost for me was joining a group for blind writers in 2008 where the encouragement and helpful critiques really brought my writing on in a big way, thanks to Gladys and Elisabeth for everything they shared and taught me. Their support has helped me to find the courage to put this book together. Ladies, you've been telling me to do this for years, and my total gratitude is yours.

To all who have decided to dip into this book of poetry and prose, my sincere thanks. If some of what you read can make you laugh, cry, or just think, I'll have created something special.

Katie Myers
July 2019

***

Songs for Singing

Record Story

It all started in 1974 when *BBC Radio Newcastle* began broadcasting a gospel programme called *Songs for Singing* on Sunday mornings.

I enjoyed the mix of music that the DJ, Frank Wappat played over the hour-long programme, and tuned in regularly. Then inspiration struck, as it so often does with me, and I sat down and wrote a gospel song reflecting the title of the programme. Contacting Frank, I asked if he'd like me to send him the song, but apologised for the lack of sheet music, as it wasn't part of the music lessons I'd ever got to grips with. He said it wasn't a problem, but could we meet at his *Mission* in Byker as he'd like to hear me sing it.

Almost before I knew it, we were in the recording studios at *Radio Newcastle* with an organist, drummer and the guitarist who I worked with for several years after that. Then there it was - a freshly minted single with my name on it!

SONGS FOR SINGING – CATHY WILKIN

A thrill, an achievement and a dream come true. This led to Frank asking me to appear at venues all over the north east when we took the show on the road. The biggest moment was the first time I stepped on to the stage at Newcastle City Hall, knowing there were 2,500 people out there. Then the show began, and all of those voices sang the chorus to my song! I can feel the emotion again just writing about it.

Here's that song that became a legend in its own lunch time, smiles: written for gospel show of same name and sung many times at the concerts known by the same name. It was very exciting to hear so many people joining in the chorus at the City Hall Newcastle when we did live shows!

Songs for Singing

Sing a song make it long
Make it last all your life
Sing it loud, sing it clear, sing it strong
For in music there's praise and in words there is hope
So, I'll sing to him all my life long

(Chorus)
Songs for singing when I'm happy
And my cares have been released
Songs for singing when I'm sad and so forlorn
I will listen to his counsel
And he'll give me once again
Songs for singing when my spirit is reborn

When you're lost on the way
And there's nothing you can trust
He will come with his light bright as day
There'll be joy all around
Then you'll clearly hear the sound
Of songs for singing as you wend your homeward way

(Chorus)
Songs for singing when I'm happy
And my cares have been released
Songs for singing when I'm sad and so forlorn

I will listen to his counsel
And he'll give me once again
Songs for singing when my spirit is reborn

Songs for singing when my spirit is reborn
(ending on high note)

[We asked Katie for her interpretation of the phrase, *'In words there is hope'* from her song, and she explained how it so relates to her writing herein...]

There is a wonderful feeling about a comment made by someone who reads your latest scribbling and you hear: *"Oh, I love this, it's great. You really captured the mood here!"* Being very self-critical, it's what I want to hear, but I also want to hear the words, *"Have you thought about changing that to...?"* or *"A little edit here might make it flow better?"*

These are the kinds of words that give me hope that my writing may find and hold a wider audience. Although I've been on the writing journey for a few years now, I'm still learning, and you don't know how much it means to have constructive criticism, which for me translates into:

'In words there is hope!'

'Songs for Singing' including the lyrics *'In words there is hope'* are © Cathy Wilkin/Katie Myers as originally written circa 1975.

***

Publisher's Overview

Katie's publishing journey has explored early memories of her creative writing beginnings, as well as her transition into the 'mind movie' world of visualisation, or 'seeing without lamp oil' as she coins it.

Through the kindness of Bob Lyons, I was pleased to be able to reunite her with a rare recording of the *Songs for Singing* (record) so that we could all share her '*In words there is hope*' message, that is so relevant today. It's been a very emotional ride as all the little gems of Katie's resilience and cheerfulness have been revealed along the way.

Additional thanks go to Gina Piears Whittle and Yve Collins for maintaining sanity and calming my frazzled nerves!

I do hope you enjoy Katie's compilation which is just a fraction of her thoughts, aspirations and writings; in fact, a true *Smattering of Smitterings*.

John Chenery

***

1: A Wiggle and A Giggle

Giggles, titters, smiles

guffaws, chuckles, howling loud

medicine that's free.

A Scottish Dream

I'm off to Scotland to buy me a kilt
Then talk with a swagger, walk with a lilt.

For learning the bagpipes, I have a yen
Imagined droning around every glen!

Take up Haggis hunting, such a delight
Scouring the hills until quite late at night.

Living on Mars bars, deep fried so ye ken
I may have a salad now and again.

Porridge with oats that put hairs on your chest
The buggers poke through the holes in my vest.

The dirk in my sock is cutting my nails
I sit in the pub tell outrageous tales.

Of battles I fought, people I've beaten
They'll never know, 'twas pie contest eating.

I'd travel abroad, sing nostalgic songs
While under my kilt I'm wearing a thong.

This helps bring genuine tears to my eyes
"More, more give us more," the crowd cheers and cries!!!

Then I wake up in my warm cosy bed
These silly lines going round in my head.

I'll pass them along, I'm not a hoarder
Two of my friends live over the border.

Taking the Biscuit

To dunk or not to, that is the question,
Could it be better for our digestion?

I spread my enquiries far and wide,
The answer's not easy, there is a divide.

Asked among family, friends - even strangers
Noticed with dunking there does comes a danger.

Of half of it falling into your tea,
Now this has regularly happened to me.

I've lost it - my biscuit - my shoulders slump,
My drink now consists of a big soggy lump.

Spoon ready to trawl, my happiness fled,
Forget it, I'll make a fresh cup instead!

Butcher Chicken

We had a takeaway last week,
Sometimes we're in the mood.
There is a lovely Chinese shop,
With friendly staff, good food.

My husband has a House Chow Mein,
Me, I like to ponder,
On all the different types of dish,
Decisions taking longer.

Sometimes I like a House Fried Rice,
With Tangy Curry Sauce.
Maybe I'll have an Egg Foo Yung,
Without the sauce, of course.

Prawn crackers used to leave me cold,
Quite crunchy but so bland.
These are prawny and five spicy,
They're not long in my hand.

My choice is crispy chicken balls,
With sweet and sour sauce.
My mind was made up in advance,
Who cares how much it cost?

The food arrived, dished out with speed,
And landed on the table.
If chicken balls were all that size
Their walk would be unstable!

Body Bits

They wander southwards, east and west,
These poor old sagging ageing breasts.

What once was perky, lithe, alert,
Now creep towards my stretchy skirt.

Once brave and braless ex-young thing,
Now shops around for scaffolding.

From younger muscles taut and tight,
When lying down, one's left, one's right.

Stretch marks abound without a gap,
And bits of skin that overlap.

Thighs that look like orange peel,
That no young stud would kill to feel.

I even checked out on the phone,
Just how they use that silicone.

And then my husband held me near,
And said, I really love you dear.

So, as the mirror I can't see,
I'll live my life as Young Old Me!

Chocolate

I'll have that chunk of chocolate
No, that bit's even bigger,
And now I feel really guilty
Cos it's so bad for me figure.

I've never been the greyhound breed
All sleek and full of curves,
And as for people like that
Well they get right on me nerves.

Don't get me wrong I'm curvy
Though it all feels out of place,
And don't ask about me waistline
There isn't any trace.

These days it's more a wasteland
With that sliding south sensation,
While in the bath I feel my tum
Could be an island constellation.

So I'll have that piece of chocolate
And another bit as well,
For as it melts upon my tongue
I'm in heaven, can't you tell?

Handle with Care

Every day is different. It's lovely just now, they're all asleep and I love it when the house is quiet. What's that, you don't understand?
Well, take yesterday...

There was a party and it felt like the world had descended on our little part of it. I was minding my own business when along comes this bloke, full of, well, something, grabs and twists me, gives a mighty heave and cracked me bottom off the wall. My missus wasn't too happy with him, I could tell by her voice. She pulled me away from the wall, and gently rubbed my backside, it did ease things a bit. Gave me a chance to have a look at the table, they call this the dining room, anyway, I've not seen this much food since Christmas.

Now where was I, oh yes...

Next thing, a teenager comes in and starts swinging on me, I was so dizzy I was glad when she stopped. I don't know if you've ever experienced long nails...well it wasn't funny.

As if that wasn't bad enough, I'm being handled, excuse the pun here, by a set of sticky fingers grabbing and twisting, we were already open, so he wasn't wanting to get in, just getting on my flipping nerves. When his mother dragged him away squealing, I felt horrible, covered in slime and goo.

Missus got a damp cloth and carefully wiped me over and buffed me with a nice soft cloth. I love these precious moments with her, she cares so much.

Too much according to the mister, he says she's, now what was it, oh yes, house proud. Nobody asks me how I feel about it, if they did, I'd tell them how much I love to be polished and buffed. They wouldn't go out looking anything but smart, so why should I hang around here looking scruffy and tatty?

I hear footsteps, the house must be waking up. Yep, here comes little feller, oh no, he's got a car in his hand, why try to open me with that in your hand, watch out, you'll scratch me... *"Ouch!"*

Now he's opened the door to the garden, ahh, that breeze is nice. I look at the handles on that door sometimes and wonder if they'll change me for that sort. Missus said never. In fact, she bought handles that were like me but a bit more streamlined but just as bright and shiny. She polishes them too.

I can't see who's coming, but I can hear heavy footsteps so it's probably the mister, yep, *"Hey gerroff!"* Why do they have to grab and hang on to me when they want to make a point?

Well at least he does... *"Ow, ease up, it's not me you're mad with!"*

Apparently little feller's in the bad books for something he's done. Oh dear, nice start to the day. He's dragged him inside, closed the doors and little feller's crying. Perhaps the missus will give him the soft cloth treatment - and here she is, right on cue.

Mister's rumbling at her, and she's not happy with him, and the sobs are getting to me. There goes the front door slamming, thank goodness the mister's gone out for the day. Little feller's calmed down and the missus is talking to him. She's got a lovely voice.

We have a lot to put up with really. There are hands of all different sizes, some angry, others soft and gentle. Little hands might be very sticky or just love to fiddle with me and try to see their reflection in me.

Here's the missus, she's got her coat on. Gently she holds me and pulls me until the door is closed. Little feller has his coat on, oh they're going out.

Time for forty winks.

***

2: Elemental Journeys

Wind, snow, rain, sleet, sun

blusters, swirls, falls, stings, soothes, bronzes

reflecting seasons.

Ice Age

*'This was written when children were allowed, to be children.
Before health and safety reared its head. Memories of times having
fun, getting bruises and enjoying being young.'*

Oh, the memories I treasure
Of us sliding together
Over ice on the shiny black ground
And the pain in your bottom
That so soon was forgotten
As we queued up again to go round

Now the playground was busy
As we spun and got dizzy
Precious time before teachers would drone
Many snowballs were flying
And some children were trying
To make a new slide of their own

9

Duty teachers stood huddled
Looking cold and befuddled
Hands in pockets, in gloves or up sleeves
All we saw were stern faces
On which were no traces
Of the children that they used to be

Then the blast of a whistle
Like the sting of a thistle
Caused every child's joy to dispel
We lined up in our forms
Marching into the warm
Listening hard for the end of school bell

Memo to the Weather

To Whom it may concern:

It has come to our attention
We're very sad to say,
That the past few days' performance
Has been lax in every way.

It's been rain instead of sunshine,
Strong winds instead of breeze,
We have to note the populace
Is really quite displeased.

A week into the month of May -
Our heating's coming on,
Please consult your calendar,
As all your dates are wrong.

The month of April's showery
But May's meant to be nice,
So, get the job done properly -
As we won't tell you twice!

Song of Seasons

Now summer's golden mantle shed
She bows to autumn's chill
That frosts each leaf and hazel hedge
Each tree so bare and still.

For all the raiment they possessed
In gold and russet brown,
Were lifted by the wind's caress
And whispered gently down.

Their silhouette by setting sun
In barren splendour stand,
As shadows lengthen, fade - are gone,
And darkness steals the land.

Then flurried by a gentle breeze
Come snowflakes tumbling down,
So, winter settles in the trees
As light as thistledown.

Then winter's cruel season bites
With howling winds and rain,
And silvered in the moon's clear light
Lie icy rutted lanes.

Then suddenly, the lark's clear song
Proclaims the birth of spring!
The days grow soft and warm and long
New life in everything!

Spring in the Air

The shops have mostly closed today,
Whatever have folk been doing?
If they had any sense at all,
There'd be much billing and cooing!

For that's what all the birds will do,
Now that spring has sprung in the air,
Flying round with love in their hearts -
Like they really don't have a care!

Some things need to be private though,
When courting gets really intense.
Find somewhere safe to do it please
As we've got a wobbly back fence!

Birth

A little bit of sunshine
Came shyly to my room,
It peeped around the corner
And brightened up the gloom.

I felt its warmth embrace me
All winter I'd been cold,
But now we're moving into spring
Or so I have been told.

I stretched and yawned, and stretched again
And pushed with all my might,
And pushed a little further
Now that I could see daylight.

I popped my head out cautiously
It all seemed very calm,
Some tiny drops of rain splashed down
A soft and gentle balm.

I stuck my head out further
And the birds began to sing,
The sweetest sound I ever heard
The signalling of spring.

***

3: Mystical Musings

How the darkness taunts

do lights dim, shadows move - crawl

are demons unchained?

Betrayed

They bobbed into the cove at night, with many a quiet curse,
Their movements swift, their fingers cold, the weather getting
worse.

As soon as every keg had gone, they rowed back out for more,
The deep black darkness was their friend, they asked for nothing
more.

Than to evade the customs men, and serve a term inside,
For all of these red-blooded men, loved laying with their brides.

But one turncoat grew loose of tongue, was sworn a bigger ration,
He'd thought to turn his brothers in, they showed him no
compassion.

Up to the inn they went that night to bluff it out he'd tried,
A fight ensued a shot rang out, and on that spot he died.

Sometimes upon the witching hour, in the darkest dregs of night,
You'll see his ghostly widow's hand, searching by lantern light.

Chills

Black is the wing of a raven,
On this Eve there is no haven.

For it is said, ghosts of the dead,
Bring mischief and mayhem and dread.

From the depths of a grim graveyard's gloom,
Figures arise from aged old tombs.

Malevolence lurks everywhere,
Spawns hopelessness drenched in despair.

Mirrors trap souls who have passed,
Do you feel the chills of a draught?

Your candle flame flares and then dies,
The air fills with unearthly cries.

A shape at the window, you scream –
Is this just a nightmare, a dream?

Eyes widen, your heart beats and teeters –
You jump as you glimpse...trick or treaters!

Confusion

'Written while going through that dark depression that visits a lot of people, but I came through with the help of a wonderful therapist. I also added a large helping of determination.'

There's something come to live inside that stops me being me,
It makes me unpredictable, makes me feel so unreal.

It's using up my Head Space and not paying any rent,
After scavenging for what it wants, it leaves me drained and spent.

Bed in the morning clings to me, dreams wake me up at night,
It's so truly bad this feeling - it's one I plan to fight!

I feel like Greta Garbo did, *'Vonting to be alone'* -
Spin round - I'm feeling chatty and gabbing on the phone.

So many tears have flown of late - quick I need a plumber!!!
To fix two brand new washers, so do you please have a number?

Its cards are marked, it won't reign long - I'll kick it into touch,
Just watch me jump - stamp - trample it, for I love my life too much!

Familiar

Glinting amber chips
Watching the old crone at work
In the black of night

Adding its magic
To the spells being woven
This familiar

Understanding all
This sleek sure-footed feline
Guards the mysteries

Devils accomplice
Creates death on stealthy paws
Merging with the night

Mist

Twisting writhing shapes
Drowning hedge field and furrow
In pale eerie light

Tattered grey ribbons
Hanging shroud-like from branches
The sky presses down

Silence is muffled
No joy lives in this half world
Only the mist moves

Light glows in the east
Mist retreats as sunlight grows
Warming comforting

Unmasked

The flaming torch illuminated each pale, apprehensive face, as she glided past. A nervous giggle was stifled and turned into a cough. So deep was the silence that her cloak could be heard rustling as she moved.

Finally, she glided into the centre of the room and in a clear voice said…

> *"I declare you to be witches and warlocks all,*
> *There's none here that are held in thrall,*
> *and now a sacrificial maid,*
> *upon the altar shall be laid."*

With that she pointed to a tall witch wearing a cloak of black and silver whose smile was a thin cruel line, the nose curved, eyes large and staring.

As she stepped towards the tall figure holding the torch aloft, Amy felt an overwhelming sense of unreality wash over her like a tidal wave, and those eyes...

They turned, walking past the still watchful faces of the crowd, stopping at a white covered altar on which the victim was forced to lie face down.

A Smattering of Smitterings

Tall black candles burned in huge candlesticks at the head of the altar. Serpents coiled and writhed around the stem - flames reflected brokenly in the water placed at the head of the alter.

"You know how you must earn your freedom?" enquired the witch standing at the foot of the alter.

There was an imperceptible nod from the prone figure.

Suddenly the pointed hat was thrown aside followed by the caricature of the evil face, which fluttered to the floor.

The tension was released with shouts of encouragement from around the room as the blonde head was immersed, time after time, finally emerging, spluttering and laughing but without an apple.

"Punishment for your failure will be to wear the mask forever," decreed the tall witch. *"Now it is open to all."*

The blonde girl picked up her hat, dried off her face, put on her mask, and re-joined her friends.

"So, no change there then," one girl teased, *"I didn't think that mask made much difference to your looks."* There was a lot of good-natured laughter around the group.

A young warlock put his arm round Amy and grinned at her. *"Are you ready for a drink?"* he asked, *"And will it be bats' blood, or a passion potion?"*

She giggled, as the neck beneath her mask turned pink, *"I'd like a passion potion please, Mark, and make it a double. I might need it later."* Her neck turned redder, as she giggled some more.

He went off for the drinks, while Amy chatted to one of her friends. Suddenly she had the uncomfortable feeling she was being stared at. Turning slowly, she saw the tall figure of the witch, still carrying the flaming torch, staring straight at her.

"Amy, are you ok?" It was the voice of her friend, coming from, what seemed to be, a long way off.

Next thing she knew, someone had pushed her down onto a chair, and she had a glass of water in her hand.

"Are you ok, Amy?" Mark was by her side.

She nodded, although, she still felt odd and couldn't seem to find her voice.

"It's a bit hot in here," her friend said helpfully. *"You'll have to ditch that mask, if you've got plans to drink the water."*

Amy dropped the hat on the floor and tried taking off the mask. *"I must be too hot, the rubber's sticking to my face. Anyone find me a straw?"*

Mark hovered beside her, as the group thinned out, most of them drifting towards the dance floor.

The tall figure of the witch could be seen walking between groups of dancers, and Amy would look up every now and again. each time, catching the dark, mesmerising eyes meeting hers, and with every glance, the sense of unreality growing stronger.

"It was a good night" Mark said, drawing Amy close, as they walked home, calling good night, as groups of friends peeled off in different directions.

"Now, can I have that kiss you promised me earlier?" he asked, turning her towards him. *"Let's have this mask off, so I can see how gorgeous you are."*
He reached for the mask and paused, *"You were hot in there. It's really sticking."*

"I'll do it." Amy began trying to pull off the mask.

A shrill laugh came from behind them, making Amy jump.

"Gorgeous, was she?" a mocking voice called from the shadows.

Amy tore desperately at the mask, which suddenly didn't seem like a mask anymore.

"Mark, help me. I don't know what's happening. Help me!"

She implored, putting out a hand which seemed to have grown talons and appeared older than before. She screamed loudly, tearing franticly at her face.

"I said your punishment was to wear the mask for all time. Did you not believe me?" asked the tall figure gliding towards her.

The witch cackled once more. Amy felt herself plunging into oblivion, as her lips sealed to the mask forever.

***

4: Squishy Wishes

Hello, I've missed you

say it with a hug or kiss

a hand gently held.

A Little Gift

It's Christmas Eve - the gifts are wrapped,
Family's been invited!
The tree is sparkling fairy lights
Kids beyond excited!

A carrot's left for Rudolf's treat,
Santa gets his sherry,
The many homes he visits means,
He ends up very merry!

The angel on the Christmas tree
Looks down from pride of place,
Bestows a silent blessing on
Each eager wond'ring face.

Everyone is praying for
A silent holy night,
Where peace abounds and love shines out,
Where fear and doubt take flight.

Then magically at stroke of 12
A message will appear,
To wish you joy and happiness
From me to you my dears!

Bouquet

When you care for someone
Who's very far away,
What can bring you closer,
Is to think of them each day

And if each thought I'm sending
Were turned into a flower,
You'd have a beautiful bouquet
Every single hour.

Wedding Wishes

There's a special kind of magic
That surrounds a wedding day.
It's full of hope and promises,
New things to come your way.

The vows and wedding rings exchanged,
The photos have been taken,
You hold each other close and know
Your love cannot be shaken.

You move together daily
Throughout the months and years.
You'll have happy, and some sad times
There'll be sunshine, and some tears.

So, keep the fire in your hearts
That sparked this magic time,
And may its warm light stay with you
May your footsteps always rhyme.

Hug-a-thon!

There's a hug inside people, whether younger or old,
You will know when it's needed -whether gentle or bold.

There's a hug for our children when a dream's bad at night,
They're so scared and need comfort, as it's far from daylight.

There's the kind that is given when your friend has good news,
Or the comforting kind when she's drowning in blues.

You've not met for ages and you wrap yourselves tight,
You're going to bed now, and you hug him goodnight.

You don't know how you're feeling - it's just one of those days,
But a hug from a loved one - you'd be really amazed!

There's a man hug, it's needed between father and son,
Or between happy team-mates when the game's good and won.

So now you see hugging has a great part to play,
I'd like to prescribe you a hug every day!

Love's Place

'Dedicated to my beautiful Mum when she passed.'

I bring a gift - a place for you
That holds your hearts desires.
A room to soothe the weary mind,
You'll find love waiting there.
The golden glow of crackling flames
Meet in every corner.
Reflecting on the silver frames
That feed nostalgic eyes
And mingle with the heady scent
Of red roses weeping softly.
On darkly lustrous wood
Close by the fragile hands
That draw the drapes of richest wine
Against the nights cold stare
Then move to douse the flickering lamps
Till shadows dance no more
Soon trusty darkness tiptoes in
And leads you down towards
Embracing folds of silken sleep
Deep in a gift of love.

***

5: Paws for Thought...
And Other Mewings and Flutterings

Soft hide, gentle hands

soothes man and pet, become one

baby squirms, rapture.

Tub of Delight

Chubby he squats in the bath
hands busy in the water
splayed splashing star fish fingers
crowing with delight.

Crab-like movements with his arms
pale shiny with water drops
swimming down, reaching bottom
gurgling with delight.

Immersed limbs frolic, caper
wriggling slippery eels
palms smacking splashing with glee
toes waggling with joy.

Clean, shrimp pink from head to toe
frothy water rocking still
he's lifted, a cry, it's over
warm fluffy towels.

Aftermath

Hello - my name is Munchkin,
I'm a very pampered pet.
I live with feline Cleo,
Oh, how can I forget?

My mistress is a film star,
Dolores her stage name.
Doris Hogg was left behind
So, she could rise to fame.

She loves to throw a party,
Her dresses are revealing;
Her hair gets done in smelly stuff,
The grey bits need concealing.

There was much ado last night,
With wine and food aplenty.
Party guests from everywhere,
I counted more than twenty.

Now they're gone there's nothing left,
Except some empty platters.
I spy with my tiny eye,
A plate with salty crackers.

Some chicken, my favourite prawns,
And look - a plate of beef!
Mummy dear comes marching in
"Munchy you little thief!"

She picks me up, and holds me tight,
Against her abundant chest.
I snuggle in, and lick my lips,
It's the place I love the best.

Butterflies

Vivid earth angels
so fragile, so fair
waltzing with flowers
their nectar to share

In cottage gardens
warm meadows, green dells
finding their pleasure
in cowslips, harebells

Drifting on breezes
a short life but full
every sweet blossom
their thirst will annul

Tiny earth dancers
their colours like gems
flirting with beauty
on slender green stems

One and One is One

'Celebrating the happy memory of my first guide dog.'

Four paws to freedom
that's what she meant
coat black and glossy
loved where she went

Cuddles and snuggles
my brown eyed girl
going with dad now
tail's in a whirl

Long walks and free runs
down at the park
or at the seaside
dodging waves, such a lark

Running in soft snow
flat on her back
paws waving madly
get back on track

Proud in her harness
we were a team
working together
creating a dream

Now she's a memory
my beautiful friend
two were one unit
a perfect blend.

Counting Sheep

I'm wide awake, it's 2 am
In my head there's too much spam

I counted sheep, but they arrived
Some in hard hats, more could drive

They carried hods, wheeled wheelbarrows
Put up buildings tall and narrow

Some smoking fags, some other's pipes
The female ones had pinkish stripes

Cement mixers, hods of bricks
Some sheep show-offs, performing tricks

This exercise to make me sleep
Has made me laugh, stuff counting sheep

Next time I see that whole workforce
I want them cooked with much mint sauce!

Sparrow Talk

Hey Dad, look at me, I'm doing it, I'm flying, weee, oh yes, this is fun. I was scared when I realised, I had to fly to get my food, but now I've got the hang of it...nearly.

Woe, nearly went into that big thingy, what did you say it was? Oh, a shed, where the human keeps all his stuff. I'll just land on top of it and have a little rest.

Oops, sorry mister human, I didn't mean to do that, but it's so exciting, you won't know what it's like until you try it...oh of course you can't. You're too big and heavy and you don't have wings.

I've seen big things with wings in the sky, but Dad says they're called planes and they fly humans to other places. We can do that all by ourselves, that makes us cleverer than them.

Oh oh, next doors cat is down there looking up, time to get moving again...I'm frightened. What if I don't fly and end up as cat food? I know Mum, I have to be big and brave, well little and brave. Here goes - and up we go. Yay, now you can't get me cat, you can't jump this high. I'll just land on this wire, oh look, there's that pretty bird that's been around here for the last few days. She's landed next to me, this is nice. I'll just fluff my feathers and do my little dance.

She tells me there's food just over there, so we fly across together and she's right, it's more food than I've seen in ages. We're side by side on a kind of flat thing with food hanging off it.

Now she's gone off to have a drink, that looks good, once I've finished here, I'll go and join in.

Oops, everyone's disappearing, it's a warning, quick, where can I hide? My lady friend's chirruping at me, there she is, move quickly. Oh oh, it's a massive bird...oh no, it got one of the starlings.

This is a good place, hope my friend is all right, oh there she is *"Hey, look I'm over here."* Can she hear me, I might have to shout a bit louder? She's flying around here now, I'll chase her and...cheeky sparrow, that's my lady not yours. I'm flying round her and she seems happy.

She comes and joins me in our cosy spot and agrees it's a great place for a nest. I'm so happy I soar up into the sky, coming back down I'm not concentrating and – blam what was that? *"Ouch my beak!"* There's a human looking at me, and its beak is curved up instead of down. I don't want to do that again. I fly back and see she's already started gathering things together to start our nest.

***

A Smattering of Smitterings

6: Smatterings of Smitterings

Life as a patchwork

all events stitching into

a miscellany.

Beginnings

Another key, a brand-new lock
It's time to open wide
Another page, a different book
Now time to look inside.

Some brand-new hopes, some newer dreams,
They must be yours to keep
Some battle scars, hostilities
It's time to bury deep.

It's in the past, it is no more
So, leave it all behind.
Give love and joy, give care, concern
Above all else, be kind.

Brexit Lament

I'm suffering Brexaustion,
I think most of us are.
Will the torment ever end?
Will the door be left ajar?

Can't they think about the folk
Who put them in to rule?
Realise without a deal
Britain will be a fool?

Once we were great, had power,
But they've given it away.
As for the House of Commons -
They're just like kids at play.

All they can do is argue,
About whose fault it is,
While the likes of you and me
Are thrown into a tizz.

I want it to be over -
Please make the right decision -
Until that day, if it comes
I'll view them with derision.

Chaos!

I love bank holiday weekends
and all its expectations.
The planning and the shopping,
with all its small frustrations.

You book a plane to go abroad
then air traffic goes on strike.
It really might be quicker
to buy yourself a bike.

As for travelling on the roads -
a pleasure I've forgotten.
Couldn't stand the tarmac trail
Or picnics getting sodden.

Service stations rip you off
and all the kids are bleating.
"I want some sweets, want some pop,"
the joys of cash are fleeting.

The trains are full, lines are closed,
there's always a diversion.
Helicopters would be nice
for family excursions.

So, I sit here in my house,
with my things all close to hand.
I just know that this weekend
will be really - really – grand!

Bond and Me!

I stood close up to Bond last night,
shaken and a little stirred.
May I have a photo of you,
with you next to me, he demurred.

So I moved a little closer,
then I heard the great *Skyfall*.
The cameras clicked; the crowd went mad
I was struck by a *Thunderball*.

"I'm sorry," he said, *"I'm leaning,*
I don't want to hit the deck.
It's down to the fans who love me
hanging too tight around my neck."

A woman moved in behind him
with a roll of tape and set about,
dragging him back to the upright,
this Daniel Craig cardboard cut-out!

Old Bones

It's a world of gadget chargers
There's so many I get lost,
And as for what they're charging us
I don't want to count the cost.

There's a charger for the *iPad*
The *iPod* and *iPhone*,
The only thing we cannot charge
Is our tottery old bones.

There's a charger for a smart car
Just plug it in the wall,
Don't forget to charge your mobile
Or you can't text or call.

There's a charger for your laptop
And one that's in your car.
I've got one for my toothbrush
Though my teeth sit in a jar!

There's a thing that makes deliveries
I think it's called a drone,
But the one thing we can never charge
Is our tottery old bones.

***

7: The Ties that Bind Us

It's all embracing

unseen, strong as ocean tides

unconditional.

A German Childhood

*'Written about a very happy time spent in Germany
when Mum and Dad were stationed there
as Salvation Army officers.'*

Where's that little girl I once knew
With neatly plaited hair?
The one that laughed so joyously
Who lived to love and share.

There they were in a photograph
The girl and a so handsome boy,
Starting their school life together
With a cone full of goodies and toys.

She collected milk for her mother
Warm bread from the corner bake store.
The pretzels were salted and doughy
She could always eat just one more.

In the winter her dad took her sledging
At the back of the house where they stayed
Mum used to watch from the balcony
Where in summer the little girl played.

It was fun making tents with a blanket
A broom shank would keep it held tight
The little girl brought out her tea set
And the dolls ate as much as they might.

It was never boring or lonely
For hours she'd play on her own,
But her make-believe friends once went shopping
Were naughty and banished back home.

She would sing for her treat at the sweet shop
Learn recorder and then the guitar
Play games in a lovely Swiss chalet
Take trips in a big cable car.

Hear cowbells so musically mellow
See snow shining bright on the peaks
Run barefoot on wide sun-warmed pavements
Be on holiday for what felt like weeks.

On the ship going home it was stormy
Rough waves and blowing a gale,
But the little girl shrieked with excitement
While the adults looked sickly and pale.

Back home she unpacked her new scooter
With blowy up tyres and a seat,
The paintwork was red and so shiny
She was proud as she raced down the street.

Now where is the boy in the picture?
Did he go on to do some great things?
Does he think of the girl he once fell for
Who now wears a bright wedding ring?

And what of the girl who liked pretzels?
Her story's not yet at an end.
Why she's here in my heart though she's older
Together we'll stay childhood friends.

Coal Pictures

Toasting by the fire
On a cold and windy night.
Watching how the flames leap
In the hearth so warm and bright.

Father brings the coal in
When the flames are just a glow.
Mother soothes with warm drinks
While the radio plays low.

Toes turn into dancers
And the spotlight paints them red.
Dressed in flickering costumes
Pretty soon it's time for bed.

Nightie warm and cosy
From its place beside the glow.
One more hug and kiss and then
It's time for me to go.

To a room that's icy
And it seems like miles away.
Down a draughty passage
To this room where I hold sway.

Now my toes are warming
As I curl up nice and tight.
Thinking of the morning
Getting dressed by firelight.

Remembering

My mum would bring me roses,
Sweet peas and Freesia too,
If I was down or sickly,
Their fragrances I knew.

I got a box from Jersey,
And opened it with glee.
Out poured the scents of Freesia,
A box full - heavenly.

Sweet peas grew in her garden,
She'd cut them just for me.
Their colour didn't matter,
Because I couldn't see.

Roses bloomed in profusion,
Their colours soft or bright.
I loved their velvet-texture,
Scents drifting in the night.

When dad died, how we missed him!
A chapter had been closed,
But each week by his picture,
One single perfect rose.

On the Beach

'So many ice creams, sandy sandwiches
and paddling while the sun shone.
Happy days!'

Dads with trouser legs rolled up,
Mums in light print frocks.
Wiggling toes into the sand,
Ditching shoes and socks.

Getting changed into my cossie,
Mum holds up a rug.
Dad's busy with the deck chairs,
Asks Mum, *"Where's the grub?"*

I love to go paddling,
When we're at the beach.
Sometimes the tide's far away,
Sadly, out of reach.

Ice-cream vendors selling cones,
Sandwiches that drip,
Wandering in the open air,
Eating salty chips.

The music from the fairground,
Screams of joy and fright -
Is sounding so exciting,
Can we go? - We might!

Next, we're in the sound and lights -
Music's loud, thumping -
We're going on the dodgems -
Driving fast, bumping -!

Arcade's next - I have pennies!
Gazing round with glee.
Look! You can win a ring here!
Will you try for me?

Next, I'm on a golden horse,
Dad's on one nearby.
Mum is sitting with the bags,
Waves as we bob by.

On the bus going home now,
We've had so much fun.
Dad says *"My two best beauties,
You've both caught the sun!"*

Looking Back

'Happy memories of trips out, going on holiday and singing
(harmonising) with my girlfriend in the back seat of Dad's car.'

A Hillman Minx with bench seats, colour cream and grey
I laid along the back seat, when we went away

I always took my pillow, plus the kitchen sink
Then I'd pester mum and dad, to park up for a drink

A friend would sometimes join me, for our holiday
Mum and dad would always plan, somewhere nice to stay

Together in the back seat, singing Beatles songs
We'd harmonise together, as we drove along

On the beach we messed around, eyeing all the boys
Childish things were stored away, no time then for toys

That old Hillman brings me back, memories by the score
Its registration number JBR 2 4.

Still Me

'This came out of a project with our writing group. We were given the words 'Still Me' and asked to write a piece on how we saw these two words. The result was the 'photographs' I have in my head, mental pictures of various wonderful memories that littered my life.'

It's all here in this big old book, my life so far.

The cover is grainy, and the edges are worn with use. Gilt letters proclaim it to be a *Family Album*. Now, the family's all gone, and there's only me left.

Turning back the cover, I see familiar writing, Mum's hand.

"Here is a record of our lovely daughter, Catherine. All the good times we had together and all of the love we shared, all captured here forever, or for as long as somebody cares"

and she's signed it. Lovely rounded letters, no squiggles or flourishes, just plain and simple - that was Mum.

Here we are, baby pictures. Looking cute, snuggled in a pink blanket, waving a tiny fist in the air, and Mum and Dad smiling adoringly down at me. The look of love in their eyes brings a lump to my throat. Oh, and there's me with Ted, probably a year old and holding that bear like it was going to be snatched away. That rather moth-eaten reminder was found in the cupboard, when we cleared Mum's house out, that and a lot of other memories.

Oh no, me in the bath holding a big green sponge in front of myself - even then, I must have had a sense of decorum. I was trying to work out my age - probably around three years-old?

Turning the page, there's me again, a look of concentration on my face, and I can't help smiling. This is such a joyful picture! I'm standing there holding a huge ice cream cone, and my tongue is out ready for the first lick. I'd be about four there. My taste buds are imagining the sweet treat cooling the tongue on a hot day.

Ah, look! me and my recorder standing in front of the Christmas tree. That one was taken in Germany; I was six and had started school. That tree looks gorgeous, and there are some of the hand carved wooden decorations in a case in the wardrobe. Magical times!

School photographs, oh my! Looking very studious in my navy blazer, pale blue shirt, navy and pale blue striped tie with a pleated grey skirt. That was the school from hell, amazing I survived it!

A Smattering of Smitterings

Flicking through the pages, I notice the changes, as I develop from child into teenager and then, into woman and smile, as memories come flooding back.

Me and my lovely friend, Maureen, on the beach in our cossies, hers was flowery, and mine was plain blue. We stand, arms linked, and not a care in the world. I wouldn't mind a few of those days now. We were both thirteen, and really starting to notice boys. We'd read the latest girlie mag and sigh over our favourite idols. We were both Beatle mad and luckily, didn't have to fight, as I loved Paul, and she adored George.

Here's one of me sitting on the rail outside the gate house at work, wearing a navy knee length dress, with a navy and white striped collar, two tone glasses, and fair hair about collar length, looking cheekily at the camera. Can't remember who took that one, but I'd put me at about seventeen. Such caring people I worked with, and all dreamed up by that well-known writer, Charles Dickens, you think I'm kidding?

Hey, there's me ready for my first night out at a club, wearing a short psychedelic patterned dress Mum made for me, oh, and the white wet look shoes. I remember Dad's reaction,

"That's far too short for her to go out in!"

Two inches above the knee was as shocking as a Victorian lady showing an ankle in Dad's eyes, and I loved him to bits, because he cared.

Wedding photos, really, did they have to keep pictures of a marriage that ended so badly? Still, it's a nice one of me and Dad. I used to joke that the smile he wore never reached his eyes - probably thinking about the cost of getting rid of a daughter. I looked so young there, and so full of hope.

Various pictures of me and Mum, one of me, Mum, and Dad, sitting at a dinner table in a restaurant. The ex must have taken the picture. We were grinning like mad at the camera, and Mum looked a bit tiddly. She tripped on the steps, as we left. Dad caught her, and her hat tipped forward, and she giggled like a schoolgirl. We were highly amused! If I remember rightly, it was one sherry and a glass of wine with the meal. Mum wasn't used to drinking.

Richard, in his fish tank in the hospital. Those baby cots didn't look much, but it helped see what was going on inside them.

There he is, about three, looking very smart dressed, in brown trousers, white shirt, and a stripy zipper jacket, for someone's wedding.

Then, came the mutinous stage, where every photo had him pulling a horrible face, as if he didn't want to do it. Such frustration trying to get him to smile, nothing worked, so there he is, page after page of glowering child. Since becoming a mother, I now know how many boys react like that to the camera. Some of the best shots were candid ones, and my gaze is fond, as I flick through them.

Growing up, he had such a gorgeous smile! I've been told many times what a handsome lad he is. It makes me so proud, and now, I know how Mum felt.

So many people and some forgotten events, and many remembered with deep affection.

A history of growth, love and laughter, joy and pain, especially, when I remember lost loved ones. Through all those captured moments, no matter how young or old, I'm still me, and there's time for more photographs in the album of my life.

***

Dreamweaver

Dreamweaver

'This was written at the tender age of 16, when thoughts of love, romance and dreams were intertwined, and it brings my poetry journey full circle.'

A boy was at the heart of it all, my very first romance. One of those that has your head in the clouds, your heart pitter pattering, and fills your every moment with daydreams.

He was up here on holiday with his family, and when he went home to Middlesex, we wrote letters back and forth. Letters full of silly drawings, funny comments and all the stuff that has you dancing round waiting for the postman to call.

There were phone calls too. Once a week on a Sunday, me in a draughty telephone box, him snug in his home. Oh, the thrill of walking up the street and looking forward to hearing his voice again.

We did get engaged when we were 18, but it was a long-distance romance, that didn't go the distance. Happily, I still have the memories, and the poem, which turned into a song, me and my guitar, and these words:

Dreamweaver

Dream weaver
make me a dream
make me a lovely world
peaceful, serene

Make me some moonlight
tender and warm
give me some starlight
a rosy red dawn

Green grass so velvet
fragrant wildflowers
time to stand still
for long endless hours

Small dancing waterfall
cooling and sweet
a very secret place
where lovers meet

Last of my wishes
to crown my scheme
the love of my life
to perfect one dream

Dream weaver
make me a dream
make me a lovely world
peaceful, serene.

***

End Notes

For the Technically Minded

JAWS is a *Job Access With Speech* screen reader, developed for the blind and partially sighted. Katie also uses NVDA – *Non-Visual Desktop Access*.

The Record

Songs for Singing was written and sung by Cathy Wilkin (our very own Katie Myers). It formed the B-side of a 7" single record pressed by the DEROY label, hence the serial DER 1153. The A-side was *'It Took a Miracle (The Miracle Song)'* penned by Petersen and sung by Frank Wappat. The trio accompanying both singers was Roy Gibson on the organ, Denny Bell on drums, and Dave Venus on guitar.

In 1957, Deroy Sound Services offered a 'tape to disc' service of the relatively new microgroove LP (33 rpm) for 25 shillings, or the firmly established 78 rpm records. Tape-to-record transfer services were an economical way of distributing sound recordings, long before the era of the cassette tape, and much later CD!

As far as is known, Katie's record was pressed as a short production-run only, and was used solely to promote the *Songs for Singing* radio programme.

A German Childhood Poem

Note: Reference to *cone*. The Germans have a custom of presenting *a cone full of goodies* to a child on their first day at school.

A Smattering of Smitterings

Cover Blurb

The front cover image is of coloured circles created by illuminated Christmas lights. Circles of red, blue, green, orange and white overlap making mysterious defocused patterns, as though looking into another universe. The overall effect could be classed as a *smattering of smitterings*!

Front cover photo: Defocused image of illuminated Christmas lights © Miguel Á. Padriñán via www.pexels.com

The back-cover photo is a thumbnail, head and shoulders of Katie in her wedding dress. She is relaxed, but her whole face is grinning with happiness. Out of shot she is raising a glass in toast to her beloved husband Brian. Katie's fairly short blonde hair, which includes a wispy fringe, is swept back in soft layers, above her ears, and just covers the back of her neck. She is wearing an elegant black vee-neck sleeveless dress, which has short cap sheer over-sleeves. The entire dress is overlaid with narrow, red ribbon, fashioned into stylised swirls, to an almost oriental design. A short string of black jet beads sits snugly at Katie's neck. A matching bracelet on her right wrist completes the ensemble.

Katie adds, *"It was a designer dress, with a matching shrug - one of the nicest outfits I ever bought. The roses I carried were the shade of one of the colours on the dress and were 'caged' in black threading (or whatever they use), with little crystal pins in the centre of some of the roses, which smelled beautiful! It brought back some memories of a very happy day."*

Back cover photo © Vivienne Mitchinson (2011)

More from Katie

Look out for an eBook and Audio Book version of this publication.

***

L - #0238 - 120819 - C0 - 210/148/4 - PB - DID2587618